NATURE  WATCH
RHINOS

Written by
Sally M. Walker

Lerner Publications Company • Minneapolis

CONTENTS

For David, Erin, Laurie, and Jeff, because they love animals. Also, for all the people who are working to save rhinos from extinction —S. M. W.

Special thanks to the late Tom Foose (1945–2006) of the International Rhino Foundation and Karen Kane of the Rhino Trust for their help with this book

Text copyright © 2007 by Sally M. Walker

Lerner Publications Company
A division of Lerner Publishing Group
241 First Avenue North
Minneapolis, MN 55401 U.S.A.

Website address: www.lernerbooks.com

Library of Congress Cataloging-in-Publication Data

Walker, Sally M.
    Rhinos / by Sally M. Walker.
      p.   cm. — (Nature watch)
    Originally published: Minneapolis : Carolrhoda Books, 1996.
    ISBN-13: 978–0–8225–6600–7 (lib. bdg. : alk. paper)
    IISBN-10: 0–8225–6600–1 (lib. bdg. : alk. paper)
    1. Rhinoceroses—Juvenile literature. I. Title.
QL737.U63W35 2007
599.66'8—dc22   2006018983

Manufactured in the United States of America
1 2 3 4 5 6 – DP – 12 11 10 09 08 07

A black rhinoceros named Kzanzaa faces the camera at Taronga Zoo in Sydney, Australia.

REMARKABLE RHINOS

A MOTHER BLACK RHINOCEROS AND HER 5-MONTH-OLD BABY *(shown above)* calmly chew hay as I walk toward them. Suddenly, a loud noise startles them.

They wheel around and bolt away with surprising speed and grace. At a safe distance, they stop, lower their heads, pick up some hay, and continue eating.

I'm lucky to be able to stand so close to these unusual animals. The reason I can is because they live in Chicago's Brookfield Zoo. Rhinoceroses are among the world's most **endangered** animals and are rarely seen in the wild. If this mother and her son lived in the wild, the terrible truth is they would likely be killed by illegal hunters, called **poachers**. Poachers earn money by selling rhinoceros horns.

A southern white rhino mother shows her 3-month-old baby how to feed on grass. In the wild, southern white rhinos live in the grassy savannas of Africa.

Modern rhinoceroses, often called rhinos, are **mammals**, animals that feed their young with their own milk. Mammals such as rhinos that have hooves and an odd number of toes are called **perissodactyls** (puh-RISS-uh-DACK-tuhlz)

In the past, about one hundred different species, or kinds, of rhinoceroses roamed North America, Europe, Africa, and Asia. Ancient rhino species included hornless rhinos and woolly rhinos. In fact, the largest land mammals ever—an ancient species called Paraceratherium—are part of the rhinoceros group. These huge creatures

Horses, which have one toe, are related to the rhinoceros. But horses and rhinos don't look much alike, do they?

grew to more than 18 feet (5.5 m) tall and 27 feet (8 m) long!

ONLY FIVE KINDS OF RHINOS

For about 30 million years, rhinos were the most common land mammal in North America. But they all became **extinct**, or died out, about 5 million years ago. All rhinos in North American

6

zoos come from Africa or Asia or have ancestors who did.

Only five species of rhino are still alive. All are in danger of extinction. Two species—the white rhino and the black rhino—live in Africa. The other three rhino species—the Indian, the Javan, and the Sumatran—survive in Asia.

White rhinos (*Ceratotherium simum*) are the most common of the five species. They live on **savannas**. These are flat, grassy areas with scattered trees. White rhinos are divided into two subspecies.

The southern subspecies (*Ceratotherium simum simum*) can be found in several African countries. But most of them live in South Africa. The population of this subspecies is about 11,300. The northern subspecies (*Ceratotherium simum cottoni*) is found only in Garamba National Park in central Africa. This protected area is in the Democratic Republic of the Congo. Only about 10 northern white rhinos are left in the park. Only 13 others live in zoos around the world.

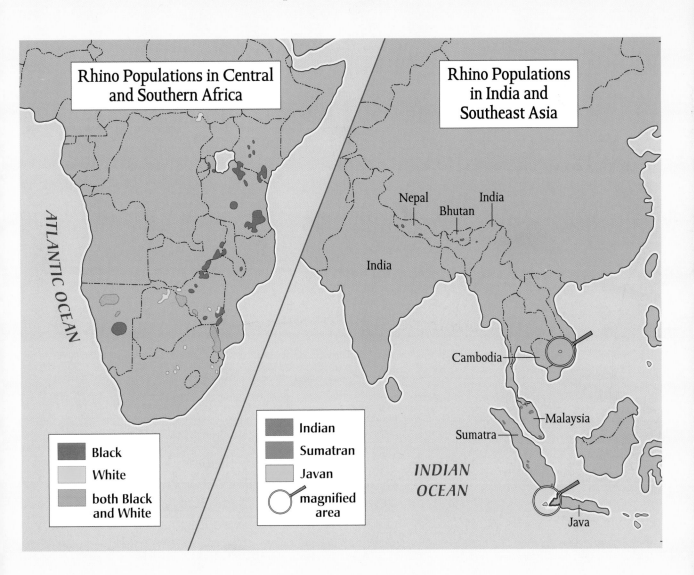

Rhino Populations in Central and Southern Africa

Rhino Populations in India and Southeast Asia

ATLANTIC OCEAN

Nepal
Bhutan
India

India

Cambodia

Sumatra

Malaysia

INDIAN OCEAN

Java

Black
White
both Black and White

Indian
Sumatran
Javan
magnified area

7

Left: In Assam, India, a mother and baby Indian rhino munch on tall grass.
Below: A rare Javan rhino roams the forests in Ujung Kulon National Park on the island of Java, Indonesia.

Black rhinos (*Diceros bicornis*) usually live in wooded areas with low shrubs and small trees. In the past, black rhinos some-times roamed the edges of savannas as well. Unfortunately, wandering across open land made them easy targets for poachers. Their numbers dwindled from about 65,000 in the early 1970s to about 3,600 in 2006.

Indian rhinos (*Rhinoceros unicornis*) prefer marshy places, especially the tall grass near rivers. They can also live on drier, grassy plains or in hilly country. In the past, Indian rhinos roamed across much of northern India. But they are quickly being squeezed off the land by poachers and by farmers who are clear-ing the land to grow crops. Most of the world's 2,400 remaining Indian rhinos live in two areas—northeastern India and nearby Nepal and Bhutan.

Javan rhinos (*Rhinoceros sondaicus*) once roamed the lush forests that cover the Indonesian islands of Java and Sumatra and parts of Southeast Asia. Javan rhinos are good climbers. They've been sighted in areas with hills measuring more than a mile (1.6 km) high. Like Indian rhinos, Javan rhinos have been pushed off the land as more people have settled there to farm. Most Javan rhinos live in Ujung Kulon National Park, on the western tip of Java. Only about 50 of them are left in the park. Another group of fewer than 10 Javan rhinos lives in southern Vietnam.

Sumatran rhinos (*Dicerorhinus sumatrensis*) are forest dwellers as well. In the past, they have roamed the Indonesian islands of Borneo and Sumatra, northeastern India, and much of Southeast Asia. That area has since been reduced to small parts of the Malay Peninsula, Borneo, and Sumatra. Sumatran rhinos are the best climbers of the rhino species. Tracks of Sumatran rhinos, like those of Javan rhinos, have been found on hills higher than a mile (1.6 km). About 300 Sumatran rhinos are still alive in the wild. But although they number more than Javan rhinos, Sumatran rhinos are considered more endangered, because poaching of the Sumatrans has increased.

Together, roughly 17,700 rhinos are left in the wild. Many of these rhinos live in national parks or in **sanctuaries**, privately owned and protected areas. An additional 1,500 rhinos live in zoos around the world.

Sumatran rhinos like this one are good climbers. Some of the slopes that they climb are so steep that a person would have to climb them on hands and knees.

PHYSICAL TRAITS

IN ADDITION TO BEING PERISSODACTYLS, RHINOS ALSO belong to a group of mammals called **pachyderms** (PAK-ih-durms), meaning thick skinned. Elephants and hippopotamuses are also pachyderms. All five species of rhinos have large barrel-shaped bodies covered with thick, gray skin. A rhinoceros's skin may be from 0.5 to 0.75 inches (1–2 cm) thick.

Rhinos vary in size from species to species. Indian and white rhinos are the largest. Indian rhinos can grow as tall as 6.5 feet (2 m) at the shoulder. White rhinos average 5 to 6 feet (1.5–1.8 m) tall. Javan and black rhinos are usually smaller and average about 5 feet (1.5 m) tall. Sumatran rhinos seem tiny when compared to the other species. Full grown, they are only 4 feet (1.2 m) tall and weigh about 1,500 pounds (681 kg).

White and Indian rhinos are the species' heavyweights. They weigh in at about 4,500 pounds (2,043 kg). This is three times the weight of a Sumatran rhino! Adult Javans usually reach about 2,500 pounds (1,135 kg). Black rhinos tip the scales at 2,000 to 3,000 pounds (908–1,362 kg).

All rhinos have three toes on each foot, but the large center toe is the one that bears most of the rhinoceros's weight. The sole of the foot is a hard, rubbery pad. Even though they appear clumsy, a rhinoceros's legs are strong and powerful. When frightened, a rhino can turn around and run faster than you could. Rhinos can gallop for short distances at speeds of 25 to 31

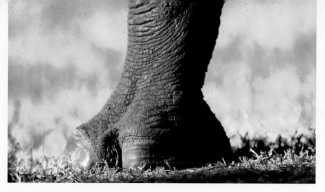

All rhinos have thick skin all over their body and three toes on each foot.

The word *pachyderm* comes from two Greek words. *Pachys* means "thick," and *derma* means "skin." So you can assume that a pachyderm has pretty thick skin.

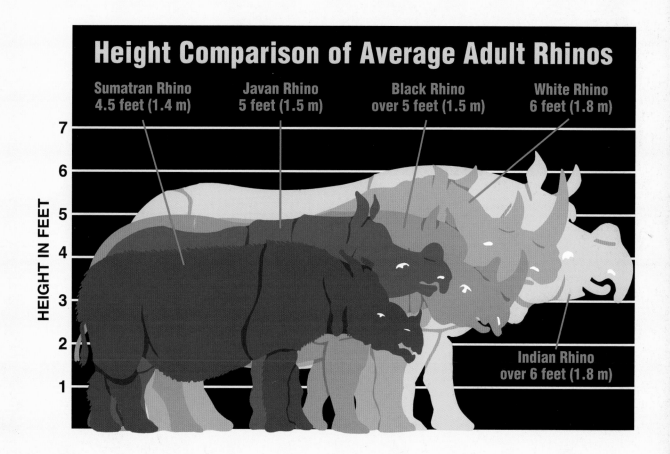

Height Comparison of Average Adult Rhinos

Sumatran Rhino
4.5 feet (1.4 m)

Javan Rhino
5 feet (1.5 m)

Black Rhino
over 5 feet (1.5 m)

White Rhino
6 feet (1.8 m)

HEIGHT IN FEET

Indian Rhino
over 6 feet (1.8 m)

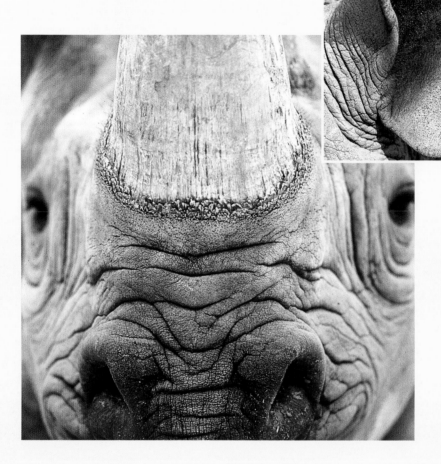

Right: Rhinos have hair on the tips of their ears. Rhinos have great hearing, perhaps because they do not have good eyesight.
Below: A rhino's horn is on top of its nose rather than on top of its head as it is with some other animals.

miles per hour (40–50 km/hr). If a rhino is angry or irritated, it may charge at whatever is bothering it—horns first!

Perhaps because their eyesight isn't too keen, rhinos have developed excellent hearing and smelling to help them sense danger. First, they swivel their ears and pinpoint the direction a sound is coming from. Then they use their noses to help them decide if it's something they need to worry about.

THE HORNS

Horns are the species' most obvious trait. All rhinos have at least one horn. Rhino horns are different from the antlers and horns of other mammals. First of all, a rhino horn grows on the animal's nose rather than on the top of its head. It grows up from the skin and is supported beneath the skin by a bony knob on the rhino's skull. The knob is larger in the Asian rhinoceros species, so their horns don't break off as easily.

Rhino horns are also different from other animals' horns because they don't have a pith, or spongy, bony center. Rhino horns are made of **keratin**, the same substance that forms hooves, hair, and fingernails. If you looked at a rhino horn through a microscope, you would see that it consists of separate hairlike strands that are packed tightly together. Because the keratin fibers are so closely packed, rhino horn is hard like other kinds of horns. Rhino horns are so hard that a charging rhino can poke a hole in a car door! If a rhino's horn breaks or splits apart, it tends to peel off in strands.

Although a horn makes a rhino look strange to us, the rhino finds it very useful. A frightened or angry rhino can use its horn to toss its enemies—such as hyenas, lions, and even people—into the air. They also use it to joust with other rhinos in tests of strength. If a fight between rhinos becomes serious, a rhino will thrust its horn upward and stab its opponent.

Two male white rhinos fight over territory in South Africa. Rhinos can use their horns to stab an opponent in a fight.

This black rhino in Kenya uses its horn to reach leaves or break down tree limbs.

Males of all rhino species, called **bulls**, are larger than females, or **cows**. Baby rhinos are **calves**.

Rhinos' horns can also come in handy at mealtimes. They use them to pull down or break tree limbs to reach the leaves to eat. During very dry weather, when many plants have died, rhinos use their horns as shovels to dig for roots or

White rhinos have two horns. White and black rhinos also have the longest horns.

water. Sometimes a horn gets broken or torn off, but it grows back.

The number and size of the horns on a rhino's nose is a good way to tell rhino species apart. Javan and Indian rhinos have only one horn. Sumatran, white, and black rhinos have two horns. White and black rhinos have the longest horns. A white rhino's front horn often grows to 6 feet (1.8 m). The longest white rhino horn on record was over 6.5 feet (2 m) long. This is longer than a tall man! A black rhino's front horn usually grows to be a little over 4 feet (1.2 m) long. This is about the size of an average 8- or 9-year-old child. The back horn of white and black rhinos is normally shorter than the front horn, perhaps only 14 to 16 inches (36–41 cm) long. Asian rhinos have much shorter horns. The front horn of a Sumatran rhino can be anywhere from 10 to 31 inches (26–79 cm) long. Its back horn may be only a short nub. An Indian rhino horn is usually from 8 to 24 inches (20–61 cm) long. The Javan rhino has the shortest horn of all. A bull's horn may reach only 10 to 10.5 inches (25–27 cm). Javan cows often have only a small knob.

Indian rhinos have only one horn. All Asian rhinos have shorter horns than white and black rhinos.

Sumatran rhinos have two horns, but they are very short compared to other kinds of rhinos.

A white rhino cow and calf eat close together. Their skin has a leathery appearance but is actually quite smooth.

Skin and Teeth

The pattern of folds on a rhino's skin is another way to identify its species. The African species don't have as many folds in their skin as the Asian species do. The folds they do have are in the lower neck area, along the tops of their legs, and near the rump. The skin of white and black rhinos has a crinkly, leathery appearance but is fairly smooth to the touch. And surprisingly, the skin on their snout and around their eyes feels just like the soft skin between a horse's nostrils—almost exactly like velvet!

An Indian rhino's skin folds across its shoulders, the top of its rump, and near the base of its tail. It has a partial fold near its neck. What makes the Indian rhino easy to identify are the knobby bumps that cover much of its body. These bumps make an Indian rhino's skin look as if it were bolted together.

A Javan rhino has a large fold of skin all the way across its neck and shoulders. It also has a fold across the base of its tail. Its skin has a crisscross pattern of wrinkles that looks somewhat scaly. It doesn't have bumps like the Indian rhino.

The Sumatran rhino is probably the easiest to identify. In addition to the large fold of skin across its shoulders, its whole body is covered with long, dark hair. This hair is especially thick when

Indian rhinos have large folds of skin across their shoulders, rump, and base of the tail.

the rhino is young. It is the only hairy rhino species. The other four species have hair only along their ears, on the tips of their tails, and as eyelashes.

Rhinos have 24 to 34 teeth, depending on their species. The exact kind of teeth they have is suited to the kinds of food they eat. All rhinos are herbivores, animals that eat plants, but they don't all eat the same ones. Savanna grasses are different from the tall, twiggy shrubs and trees that grow in forests.

All rhinos have 12 to 14 pairs of molars. These are large, ridged teeth located in the back of the mouth. Molars are used for grinding up plants. The three Asian species also have **incisors** (in-SY-zers). These sharp teeth in the front of the mouth are used for nipping grass and leaves. African rhinos don't have incisors. Only Sumatran rhinos have a sharp, cone-shaped **canine tooth** on each side of their lower jaw. Scientists suspect that they do not use their canine teeth for eating at all but for slashing opponents during fights.

Right: **A black rhino chews a twig and leaves, using its teeth to get the leaves off the branch.**
Below: **Sumatran rhinos are the only species that have hair all over their bodies.**

DAILY ROUTINE

RHINOS EAT BY GRABBING PLANTS WITH THEIR LIPS AND pulling them into their mouths. The way they do this depends on the kinds of plants they eat and the shape of their upper lip. White rhinos have a wide, square upper lip *(shown above)*, perfectly suited for ripping off large clumps of grass. In fact, it's this wide upper lip that gave the white rhinoceros its name. The "white" in its name has nothing to do with its color—white and black rhinos are pretty much the same shade of gray. "White" is really a mistranslation of the Dutch word *wijde*, which means "wide." (Dutch was one of the languages spoken by early European settlers in Africa.)

Black rhinos have a prehensile lip that helps them pull leaves and twigs into their mouths.

EATING HABITS

Black, Sumatran, and Javan rhinos are all considered to be browsers, animals whose normal diet consists of tender shoots, twigs, and leaves. These three species have a pointed upper lip called a **prehensile** (pree-HENT-sill) lip. Something is prehensile if it can grab and hold on to an object. (Your fingers are a good example.) A rhino with a prehensile lip wraps the lip around leaves and twigs, rips them off, and pulls them into its mouth. It can also use its lip to pluck fruit from a tree, pick up fallen fruit from the ground, or tear up long grasses.

Hungry Sumatran and Javan rhinos have been observed "walking down" young trees. To do this, a rhino walks up a tree until it is bent over and trapped between the rhino's front legs. When the leaves are within reach, the rhino eats them, along with any tasty fruit that may be growing on the tree. Some rhinos are strong enough to walk down trees with trunks as thick as 3 to 4 inches (8–10 cm).

Indian rhinos are considered grazers, animals that eat mostly grasses. They have a partially prehensile lip, which they fold up out of the way while they are grazing. But their prehensile lip comes in handy when they eat fruit, water plants, bamboo shoots, leaves, and shrubs. Unfortunately, Indian rhinos also like to eat young rice plants, corn, lentils, and potatoes. Local farmers grow these crops for food, so the rhinos' munching makes the farmers angry.

Rhinos spend almost half their lives eating. They usually eat during the cooler parts of the day—in the evening, at night, and in the early morning. It's dif-ficult to observe rhinos in the wild. So it's hard to know exactly how much food they eat per day. Rhinos in zoos are fed hay mixed with grains, vitamins, and minerals to keep them healthy. They eat about 1 to 2 percent of their body weight per day, or 45 to 90 pounds (20–41 kg) for white rhinos and 25 to 50 pounds (11–23 kg) for Javans.

Rhinos in the wild must search for their food. How large an area a rhino roams depends on how much food is available.

Right: Javan rhinos, like all rhinos, spend almost half their lives eating, mostly when the weather is cool. *Below:* White rhinos roam freely at a park in South Africa.

Rhinos sleep during the day. This white rhino strikes a typical sleeping pose.

When food is plentiful, the area can be small, only a few square miles. If food is scarce, a feeding area must be larger, sometimes 6 square miles (16 sq. km) or more. Browsers often roam farther than grazers, because the shrubs browsers enjoy don't grow close together the way grasses do.

SLEEPING AND STAYING COOL

The hottest part of each day is spent resting and trying to stay cool. About one-third of a rhino's day is spent resting or sleeping. Rhinos are sound sleepers. They may lie on their side with their legs stretched out. More often, they lie with their legs gathered beneath them, head upright, with their chin resting on the ground. Like horses, rhinos can also sleep standing up.

All rhinos live in warm places, so they need water regularly. They drink from 15 to 25 gallons (57–95 l.) of water a day. Rhinos can go several days without water. But they prefer to stay in an

This white rhino visits a watering hole in South Africa. Rhinos usually stay near water, which they drink as often as they can.

A rhino *(right)* wallows in the mud to stay cool. The caked mud also acts as sunscreen lotion!

area where they can drink daily. They sometimes chew succulent, or water-filled, plants if they can't get to water. Rhinos will walk from 5 to 15 miles (8–24 km) a day in order to drink. In times of very dry weather, they will dig to reach water that flows underground.

Rhinos often plop into the water and rest or sleep in it. They also splash around and swim. This behavior is particularly true of Indian rhinos, which live near rivers. Rhinos can't sweat like we do, so this helps them stay cool.

Another way rhinos stay cool is to **wallow**, or roll around, in cool, wet mud. When it dries, the muddy covering protects them against sunburn and makes it more difficult for **parasites** and insects to bite them. If no mud is available, a rhino will wallow in the dust, which probably provides some protection and gives the rhino a nice back scratch.

A rhino travels specific routes to its feeding areas and the nearest water hole. Walking to and fro each day wears a grooved path that may be as wide as 20 inches (51 cm) and as deep as 14 inches (36 cm). Rhino paths that cut through heavy plant growth are like low, green tunnels. Paths leading to water holes are considered public property. This means rhinos share them with other rhinos. But paths to sleeping and feeding areas are considered private.

Birds debug a black rhino in Tanzania. Birds often land on rhinos and eat the pests off their bodies.

DEBUGGING

Mud and dust don't keep all biting pests away, though. When it's time to debug, certain birds are rhinos' best friends. In Africa, the oxpecker, sometimes called the tick bird, lands on a rhino. It works its way around the rhino's body, eating ticks. In Asia, mynah birds help out Indian rhinos the same way. Rhinos don't even seem to mind when the birds peck inside their ears or around their nostrils. Oxpeckers also act as an alarm system. When danger approaches, the birds fly up into the air and squawk loudly. The sound alerts the rhino of possible trouble.

CALLS, SIGNALS, AND SIGNS

RHINOS COMMUNICATE USING A WIDE RANGE OF SOUNDS and body language. If a dominant bull making his daily rounds meets another bull, he growls and may curl his tail up over his back as a sign that he is upset. The bulls test each other's strength by horn wrestling *(shown above)* and charging into each other's shoulders. This establishes which bull is the strongest. That bull will occupy a dominant, or higher, social position. As long as the weaker bull doesn't challenge the dominant one, a meeting may not lead to a fight. Unless he's looking for trouble, the other (most likely younger) male chirps at the stronger bull. It's as if he's saying, "Relax, I know who's in charge." If a fight erupts, both adults roar and grunt.

This 12-day-old female Indian rhino calf only needs to cry out and its mother will pay attention.

Unless a cow has a calf, she doesn't usually mind being near other cows or young adult rhinos. Although a baby rhino's call is much quieter than a bull's, it is sure to bring a quick response from its mother. It may whine to grab her attention or squeal if it is afraid. Then mom immediately comes running.

Zoologists (scientists who study animal life) have learned that rhinos also use a "silent" call to communicate with one another. Like whales' songs, these

infrasonic sounds are below the range of sounds that humans can hear. The sounds can also travel long distances.

STRONG SIGNS

Not all rhino communication involves sound. Like many animals, a rhino bull lets others know the boundaries of his **home range**—the area in which he lives. He sprays urine on bushes, trees, grass, and rocks. African rhino bulls patrolling the borders of their home ranges spray every few minutes. Zoologists aren't sure if all male urine spraying is range marking. It's possible that it may be a kind of identifying mark. It's as if they are saying, "Hey, I've been here!" whether they're in their own home range or not.

Female rhinos also spray. But they're sending an entirely different message. Spraying urine tells bulls that a female rhino is ready to mate. She also makes a whistling sound to send her message.

Bulls tend to avoid other rhinos, when they can. In places where the amount of available space is limited, like a national park or zoo, rhino bulls put up with the presence of others.

Rhinos also mark their presence by eliminating solid waste (pooping) in communal **dung** heaps. Over time, these piles may reach 3 feet (0.9 m) high and 16 feet (4.9 m) across. A rhino's excellent sense of smell enables it to tell apart rhino neighbors and strangers by the scent of their dung. That way, a rhino can keep track of who is around. And it seems it's just as important to be smelled as it is to smell others. Wildlife observers have seen white rhinos in full gallop suddenly stop when they reach a communal dung heap, poop, and then take off running again!

A male black rhino marks its territory by spraying its urine.

Making Rhino Babies

When a female rhino is ready to mate, she is said to be in estrus. This is the time when she is able to become pregnant. Cows begin to experience estrus at about 3 years of age. But they may not have their first baby for several more years. Bulls are able to reproduce at about 7 to 9 years of age.

Courting rhinos don't murmur sweet nothings into each other's ears. Rhino courtship is noisy and sometimes even violent. Snorting, squealing, puffing, roaring, and whistling are some of the sounds courting rhinos make. Cows have been known to attack courting bulls and injure them with their horns.

Two black rhinos prepare to mate. Rhinos do not remain together after mating.

Just before mating, a bull lays its head across the cow's back. During the next day or so, the bull may mount and mate with the cow several times. But after that, they both go their separate ways. Rhinos do not remain together as a family. The bull does not help to raise their calf.

Gestation is the time a calf needs to develop inside the mother before it is born. The time this takes varies slightly among the five species. Gestation averages 15 months for black rhinos and 16 months for white, Indian, and Sumatran rhinos. Javan rhinos are so hard to find that it's almost impossible to study them.

But based on the animals' size and weight, zoologists think that a Javan rhino's gestation period is about 16 months too.

GIVING BIRTH

A rhino cow gives birth standing up and delivers one calf. Twins are very rare. Shortly before her baby is born, a cow often gets cranky. Female rhinos in zoos are normally calm and friendly with their keepers. But in the days before a baby's birth, they can become violent. They go back to their gentle manner within days, sometimes only hours, after giving birth.

A white rhino looks after her newborn calf at an animal park in Britain.

Suci, a 3-week-old Sumatran rhino, cools off at the Cincinnati Zoo in Ohio. Her mother was the first Sumatran rhino to give birth in captivity. Suci weighed about 75 pounds (34 kg) at birth. As a 1-year-old, she weighed about 900 pounds (408 kg).

In the wild, a female usually hides when she is about to give birth. She and the calf remain alone for several days. The mother probably does this for the calf's protection, since bulls sometimes attack newborn calves.

Even at birth, all rhino babies are pretty big, measuring about 2 feet (0.6 m) tall. White and Indian rhino newborns weigh 100 to 150 pounds (45–68 kg). Newborn black calves weigh 60 to 90 pounds (27–41 kg). Sumatran calves tip the scales at about 75 pounds (34 kg). (We know very little about the weight of newborn Javan rhinos.)

Rhinos are born with a smooth, flat, oval plate on their nose. At about 5 weeks of age, a horn will start to grow there. Rhino calves have the same folds in their skin as adults do. They also may have some hair on their bodies, which falls out as they grow older (unless they are Sumatran rhinos).

Baby rhinos struggle to their feet as soon as 10 minutes after birth. Wobbly at first, they are fairly steady on their legs within a few hours. Right away, calves search for one of their mother's two nipples and begin nursing. They nurse often and for several minutes at a time. So a mother rhino must be able to produce a lot of milk. For example, an Indian rhino cow produces from 34 to 44 pints (16–21 l.) of milk per day to meet her baby's nutritional needs. That's enough milk for 30 kindergartners!

This 3-month-old southern white rhino joined its mother's herd soon after birth.

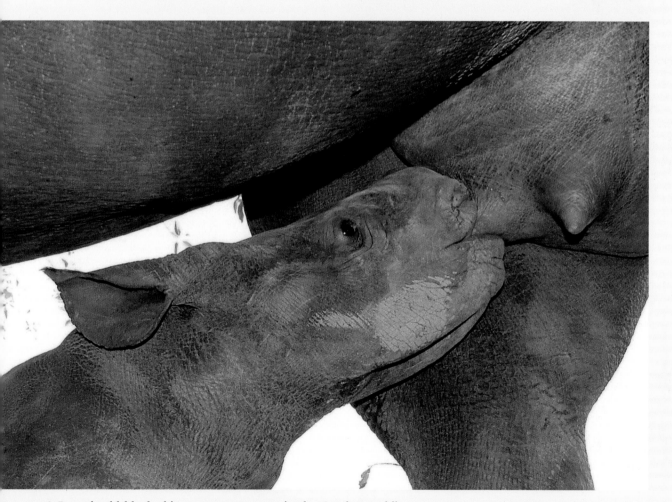

A 3-week-old black rhino nurses at a zoo in the Czech Republic.

Baby rhinos gain weight rapidly—as much as 4.5 to 6.5 pounds (2–3 kg) a day. Calves nurse for about a year. They slowly add solid food to their diet. By the end of that year, the baby will be about 10 times heavier than it was at birth. In zoos, calves as young as 2 weeks old have been seen nibbling plants, but they don't usually eat them regularly until they are a few months old.

GROWING UP RHINO

Rhino mothers are very protective of their babies and always keep them close by. Healthy adult rhinos don't really have any **predators**, or animals that hunt

Suci eats ficus leaves with her mother at the Cincinnati Zoo. Most baby rhinos in the wild don't eat plants until they are older.

A black rhino calf follows its mother in Tanzania. Black rhino mothers lead the way so they can protect the young rhino from predators.

them (except humans). But hyenas, tigers, and occasionally lions attack baby rhinos. In times of danger, a mother rhino will turn sideways so that her body blocks the predator's path to her baby. If a group of several white rhino cows and calves sense danger, the cows arrange themselves in a circle. They put their rumps toward the center and their horns pointing outward. The group of calves is in the center of the circle. Faced with the points of so many horns, a smart predator will think twice about attacking.

Black rhino mothers always make their calves travel behind them. Many zoologists believe this is because they live in a wooded, shrub-filled **habitat**, or area. A predator can easily hide in the brush and attack a baby rhino before it is aware of the danger. But an alert mother rhino walking ahead of her baby is able to handle any surprise attackers that might leap into her path.

In contrast, white rhino calves always walk in front of their mothers. Again, habitat may determine this behavior. As the mother moves along behind her calf, she has a good view of any predators that may be sneaking across the open savanna. Indian rhino calves seem to

35

Rhino calves stay with their mothers until they are 2 or 3 years old. Then they hook up with other young rhinos.

take advantage of both strategies. Very young Indian rhinos tend to follow their mothers. As they get older and larger, they shift position and the youngsters travel in front.

Calves remain with their mothers until they are about 2 or 3 years old. Sometimes they stay together longer. Females can give birth every 2 or 3 years. But if she is still caring for a calf, a cow in the wild may wait up to 5 years before mating again. When a new calf is born, the cow drives the older calf away. Over a natural life span, a rhino may have as many as 10 or 11 calves.

After leaving their mothers, young rhinos frequently join up with one or more other rhinos, usually of the same sex and about the same age. Sometimes they will tag along with an **aunt**, an older female who has no calf. They travel around together until they are ready to establish their own home ranges, usually by the time they are 5.

Rhinos in zoos have lived into their forties. Left to die of natural causes in the wild, they may live longer. Unfortunately, most rhinos in the wild are killed before they have the chance to live out a natural lifetime.

A 27-year-old white rhino gets sprayed down with water at the Budapest Zoo in Hungary. Rhinos in zoos have lived into their forties.

THE KILLING
MUST STOP

IF RHINOS BECOME EXTINCT, IT WILL BE DUE ENTIRELY TO human activity. Over the years, we have killed rhinos for their horns *(shown above)*. We have destroyed their habitats to create fields for farming and to supply lumber for the timber industry. Tens of thousands more rhinos were killed by sport hunters before rhino hunting became illegal.

During the past 30 years, however, most rhinos have been killed when poachers have cut out their horns. Rhino horn has been an ingredient in traditional Asian medicines for hundreds of years. These medicines are still used in China, Taiwan, and Korea. They treat fever, headaches, and other illnesses. Rhino conservation groups estimate that 26,000 to 36,000 pounds (11,804–16,344 kg) of rhino horn are in illegal stockpiles in China and Taiwan. Those figures alone account for about 17,000 to

24,000 rhinos. This is roughly the same as the total number of rhinos still alive around the world.

Rhino horn has also been in great demand in northern Yemen. The horns are carved into handles for fancy daggers. These are given to young Yemeni men as a symbol of becoming adults. During the 1970s, an average of 16,000 pounds (7,264 kg) of rhino horn were sold there each year. After some international pressure, the Yemeni government cracked down on horn sales. The sales of the daggers have slowed since then.

An international law bans the trade of rhino horn. Sadly, a few nations such as China and Taiwan that signed up to honor the ban aren't following it. Nations such as South Korea that didn't sign are ignoring the ban altogether.

Left: This white rhino was killed for its horn, which is used in traditional Asian medicines.
Below: Park rangers walk by the body of a black rhino killed by poachers in a park in Namibia.

Rhino horn dealers are willing to break the law. They can find buyers willing to pay an average of up to $30,000 per pound for rhino horn. That's almost five times the price of a pound of gold.

Catching poachers and dealers is one step in the fight to save rhinos from extinction. Another step is to refuse to buy goods from countries that don't crack down hard on the use of rhino products. Another need is to educate people about the seriousness of the rhino situation. Even though it may be hard, people must learn to use other materials for dagger handles. They can learn to treat illnesses with aspirin or other substances that reduce fevers and headaches.

Armed park rangers protect a white rhino at a park in Kenya.

LOOKING AHEAD

The future survival of rhinos depends on what we do to protect them. The Javan rhino population in Ujung Kulon National Park has been doing fairly well. Plans are being made to fence in one area of the park to create a sanctuary that will keep the remaining rhinos even safer.

Even though national parks are patrolled and guarded, poaching in the national parks of Nepal, India, South Africa, and Zimbabwe is still a very serious problem. Some African countries have tried to stop poachers by capturing rhinos and sawing off their horns. This is a very expensive undertaking, because rhinos' horns grow back again. Tragically, when there aren't enough rangers to patrol an area constantly, poachers kill dehorned rhinos anyway. (Even the stub of a horn is valuable.) And **dehorning** might make it harder for rhino mothers to protect their babies from predators. However, a combination of methods—hiring more rangers *and* dehorning rhinos—may be effective at saving them.

The safest places for rhinos seem to be sanctuaries. The best sanctuaries are heavily patrolled and surrounded by electric fences to keep out poachers. In these areas, rhinos are able to live and breed in safety.

Zoos are also actively working to save rhinos from extinction. The Species Survival Plan is one program that helps endangered species by breeding them in captivity. Zoologists hope to learn more about rhino reproduction to make cap-

A dehorned white rhino munches on grass. The horn will eventually grow back.

tive breeding programs even more effective. Someday maybe the world will be safe enough to release some young rhinos back into the wild.

The Minnesota Zoo is helping to save Javan rhinos in the wild by participating in the Adopt-a-Park Program. The zoo sends money (donated by visitors to the zoo) directly to Ujung Kulon National Park.

41

A Few Triumphs

Zoos and sanctuaries around the world have had some major triumphs in saving rhinos in recent years. The Cincinnati Zoo, for example, celebrated the birth of a male Sumatran rhino in 2001. He was the first Sumatran rhino to be born in captivity in more than 100 years. Since then, the cow became pregnant again and gave birth to another healthy baby in 2004. The zoo even has a one-of-a-kind program to gather money to help save more rhinos. The zoo has several adult rhinos. Using their prehensile lips and with the help of a zoo caretaker, the rhinos create unique paintings. The paintings are on sale and directly help their cousins in the wild.

Malaysia and Indonesia have stepped up their efforts of protecting the rhinos in the wild. Rhino Protection Units (RPUs) are anti poaching groups that roam forested areas. If they find a rhino in danger, the units tell sanctuary authorities. They arrange for the rhino to be moved into a protected area. The Indian state of Assam has launched a major program called Indian Rhino Vision 2020. Because of conservation efforts, the number of Indian rhinos has risen. Two of Assam's sanctuaries are severely overcrowded. The program is meant to move rhinos to other protected areas of the state. This will give the animals plenty of room to roam and breed.

Indian rhino Nikki paints using her prehensile lips with the help of a zoo caretaker at the Cincinnati Zoo. The paintings are sold to raise money to help protect rhinos in the wild.

The World Wildlife Fund has partnered with countries in many parts of Africa to increase rhino populations in protected areas. South Africa's efforts with the southern white rhino are a rousing success story. More than 100 years ago, the subspecies' population was about 100. Since then, careful management has brought that number to more than 11,000.

A baby black rhino stays close to its mother at the Metrozoo in Miami, Florida.

The park uses the money to buy supplies and equipment to protect rhinos and to pay rangers.

Conservationists estimate it will cost $60 to $100 million to save Asian rhinos and even more to save African rhinos. This money will also help save rhino habitats and all the creatures who share them. We must find ways to make this happen. The rhinoceros's future is in our hands.

GLOSSARY

aunt: a calfless adult female rhino that keeps company with one or more immature rhinos

bull: an adult male rhinoceros

calf: a baby rhinoceros

canine tooth: one of two sharp teeth near the front of the lower jaw in a Sumatran rhino

cow: an adult female rhinoceros

dehorning: the process of cutting off a rhino's horn

dung: an animal's solid waste, or poop

endangered: at risk of losing all members of a species forever

estrus: the time when a female rhino can become pregnant

extinct: having no members of a species left alive

gestation: the period of development of a calf before birth

habitat: the type of area where something lives, such as a forest

home range: the area in which an animal eats, roams, and breeds

incisor: a tooth near the front of the upper jaw in Asian rhino species that is used for cutting grass and leaves

infrasonic: a sound that is too low for humans to hear

keratin: a protein that makes up rhino horn and human fingernails

mammal: an animal that feeds its young with milk from the mother's own body

molar: a large, flat tooth in the back of a rhino's mouth that is used for grinding food

pachyderm: one of a group of animals with hooves and thick skin, including rhinos, elephants, and pigs

parasite: an organism that lives on or in another organism and usually causes its host harm

perissodactyl: one of a group of animals with hooves and an odd number of toes, including rhinos and horses

poacher: a person who hunts illegally

predator: an animal that kills other animals for food

prehensile: able to grasp something

sanctuary: a privately owned area fenced in and guarded to protect the wildlife inside

savanna: a flat, grassy area with only a few trees

wallow: to roll around, usually in mud

SELECTED BIBLIOGRAPHY

Martin, Esmond, and Chryssee Bradley Martin. *Run, Rhino, Run.* London: Chatto & Windus, 1982.

Maynard, Thane. *A Rhino Comes to America.* Danbury, CT: Franklin Watts, 1993.

Penny, Malcolm. *Rhinos: Endangered Species.* New York: Facts on File, 1988.

WEBSITES

International Rhino Foundation

http://www.rhinos-irf.org

This not-for-profit group gathers money and information to support the preservation of rhinos in the wild and in zoos. Its Rhino Rangers program is set up especially to give kids a way to help save rhinos.

Save the Rhino International

http://www.savetherhino.org

This not-for-profit group focuses on preserving rhinos in the wild. The education section of the group's website has a special part for kids.

SOS Rhino

http://www.sosrhino.org/knowledge

This not-for-profit group focuses on the highly endangered Sumatran rhino. A special part of the site set aside for kids has maps, photos, videos, and more.

FURTHER READING

Cole, Melissa S. *Rhinos*. Farmington Hills, MI: Blackbirch, 2002.

Dixon, Franklin W. *The Mystery of the Black Rhino*. New York: Simon and Schuster, 2003.

Hamilton, Garry. *Rhino Rescue: Changing the Future for Endangered Wildlife*. Buffalo: Firefly Books, 2006.

Murray, Peter. *Rhinos*. Chanhassen, MN: Child's World, 2006.

Penny, Malcolm. *Black Rhino: Habitats, Life Cycle, Food Chains, Threats*. Austin, TX: Raintree Steck-Vaughn, 2001.

Spilsbury, Louise A., and Richard Spilsbury. *Black Rhino*. Chicago: Heinemann, 2006.

Toon, Steve, and Ann Toon. *Rhinos*. Stillwater, MN: Voyageur Press, 2002.

Watt, E. Melanie. *Black Rhinos*. Austin, TX: Raintree Steck-Vaughn, 1998.

INDEX

ABOUT THE AUTHOR

Sally M. Walker is the author of many award-winning nonfiction books for young readers. She is the author of *Secrets of a Civil War Submarine: Solving the Mysteries of the* H. L. Hunley, which won the prestigious Sibert award in 2006. When she isn't busy writing or doing research for books, Walker works as a children's literature consultant. She gives presentations at many reading conferences and has taught at Northern Illinois University. Among her other books with Lerner Publishing Group are *Fossil Fish Found Alive, Magnetism, Light, Sound*, and *Electricity*.

PHOTO ACKNOWLEDGMENTS

The images in this book are used with permission of: Thomas A. Hermann/NBII, pp. 2, 3, 15 (top), 19; © Getty Images, pp. 4, 6, 16, 17, 18 (left), 23, 27, 29, 31, 32, 33 (both), 34, 37, 38, 43, 46; © Sally M. Walker, p. 5; © kevinschafer.com, pp. 8 (top), 14; © Mary Plage/Oxford Scientific/jupiterimages, p. 8 (bottom); © Ken Lucas/Visuals Unlimited, pp. 9, 15 (middle); © Dave Hamman/Gallo Images/Getty Images, p. 10; © age fotostock/Superstock, p. 11; © Tom and Pat Leeson, p. 12 (top); © Art Wolfe/www.ArtWolfe.com, pp. 12 (bottom), 21 (top); © Richard du Toit; Gallo Images/CORBIS, p. 13; © Terry Whittaker; Frank Lane Picture Agency/CORBIS, p. 15 (bottom); © Wendy Dennis/Visuals Unlimited, p. 18 (right); © Erwin and Peggy Bauer, p. 20; © Per-Anders Pettersson/Getty Images, p. 21 (bottom); © Michele Burgess, p. 22; © Royalty-Free/CORBIS, p. 24; © Kennan Ward/CORBIS, p. 25; © Jeremy Voisey/iStockphoto, p. 26; © Mike Powles/Oxford Scientific/jupiterimages, p. 28; © Yann Arthus-Bertrand/CORBIS, p. 30; Murphy, Terry/Animals Animals – Earth Scenes, p. 35; Photodisc Royalty Free by Getty Images, p. 36; © Tom Stoddart Archive/Getty Images, p. 39 (top); © Martin Harvey/CORBIS, p. 39 (bottom); © Shane Moore/Animals Animals – Earth Scenes, p. 40; © G. Ellis/GLOBIO.org, p. 41; tomuphoto.com, p. 42.
Illustration on p. 7 by © Laura Westlund/Independent Picture Service

Front cover: © Creatas/Superstock
Back cover: © Getty Images